NATIONAL
GEOGRAPHIC

Fractions Everywhere!

Jordan Paul

Fractions are all around us.

Fractions help us
share things.

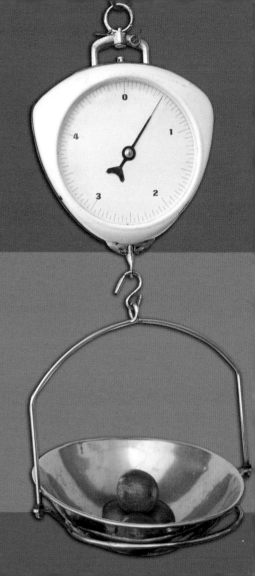

Fractions help us keep track of time.

Fractions help us measure things.

We use fractions when we eat breakfast. Mom cuts the pastry into four equal pieces. I will eat **one fourth** of the pastry.

$$\frac{1}{4}$$

We use fractions when we play a game.
There are ten marbles.
We each take five marbles.
I will have **one half** of the ten marbles.

$$\frac{1}{2}$$

We use fractions at the grocery store.
Mom weighs the apples on the scale.
The apples weigh **half** a pound.

$$\frac{1}{2}$$

We use fractions at the shoe store.
The salesperson measures the length
of my foot.
Shoes come in full and half sizes.
I wear size **ten and a half**.

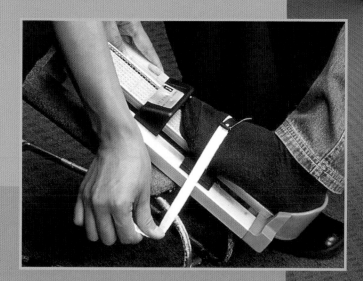

We use fractions at the doctor's office.
The doctor measures how tall I am.
I am **four and a half** feet tall.

$4\frac{1}{2}$

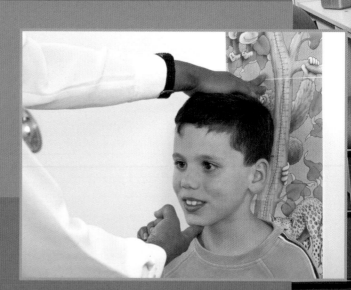

We use fractions when we watch sports. A basketball game is played in **quarters**, or four periods.
At the end of the third quarter, **three fourths** of the game is over.

How do you use fractions?